Design: Judith Chant and Alison Lee
Recipe Photography: Peter Barry
Jacket and Illustration Artwork: Jane Winton, courtesy of
Bernard Thornton Artists, London
Editors: Jillian Stewart and Kate Cranshaw

CLB 4264
Published by Grange Books, an imprint of Grange Books PLC,
The Grange, Grange Yard, London, SE1 3AG
© 1995 CLB Publishing, Godalming, Surrey, England.
Printed and bound in Singapore
Published 1995
ISBN 1-85627-588-4

THE LITTLE BOOK · OF ·

Cooking For One

A selection of tasty recipes for individuals interested in quick and easy cooking.

Grange BOOKS

Introduction

Cooking for one sounds easy, but in fact it is often easier to cook a family casserole or pie than it is to make a single portion of something tasty. It is too easy not to bother, and just make do with a sandwich and a piece of cake, or a piece of cheese and an apple. Sometimes this makes a nice change and is the appropriate thing to do, but on a daily basis it is not good for the morale, and it can lead to a poor and dull diet.

There is a side to cooking that is therapeutic and comforting. There is the planning involved, the shopping, the preparation, and finally the eating and enjoyment of something thoughtfully made. Cooking and eating good food adds an extra dimension to the day whether you are eating alone or with friends.

There are certain aspects of our high-tech modern world that actually make it far easier to shop and cook for one than could be imagined a few years ago. Firstly, there is a greater selection of foods than ever before, with a vast array of exotic fruit and vegetables, meat and fish, and spices and grains from all over the world filling our supermarket shelves. Self-service weighing scales are a great boon when buying fruit and vegetables as they enable the shopper to buy exactly the amount they require. Also, once home with the shopping the microwave can be of tremendous help in cooking vegetables and reheating previously made dishes. It was always a shame, in the pre-microwave era, when yesterday's succulent fish pie became dry after lengthy reheating in the oven. Of course, the freezer has obvious advantages for the single person, too. Delicious bakes, risottos and casseroles can be made, divided into portions and frozen for later use.

People cooking for themselves generally do not want to spend too long preparing their meals, and if they are going to cook, they want the result to be something special – that is what this book is all about. The recipes are easy to follow, simple to prepare, and each one has an extra ingredient or clever method to make the dish particularly appetising. For instance, olives are added to scrambled eggs, lemon is added to sautéed pork, green peppers and tomato go into the ham omelette, filleted fish is pan-blackened with cayenne and paprika, and pancakes are filled with apple. Thus, with today's rich and varied food supply, plus the recipes in this book to add the necessary stimulus, those who are cooking for one have no excuse not to eat an exciting and nutritious diet.

Scrambled Eggs with Olives

SERVES 1

The addition of black olives to scrambled eggs turns this simple dish into a memorable one.

PREPARATION: 10 mins
COOKING: 15 mins

---

3 eggs
2 tbsps olive oil
¼ small onion, chopped
1 small clove garlic, chopped
1 tomato, seeded and finely chopped
4 black olives, pitted and finely chopped
Butter
Salt and pepper

---

1. Beat the eggs and set them aside.

2. Warm the olive oil in a small frying pan, increase the heat to high and cook the onion, garlic, tomato and olives until all the juices have evaporated.

3. Heat a little butter in a small saucepan, add the eggs and cook over a gentle heat, stirring continuously with a wooden spoon.

4. Once the eggs are cooked, stir in the tomato

Step 3 Cook the eggs over a gentle heat stirring continuously with a wooden spoon.

Step 4 Once the eggs are cooked, stir in the tomato and olive mixture.

and olive mixture. Heat through and serve immediately.

9

Omelette Rousillon

MAKES 1 OMELETTE

Rousillon is on France's border with Spain. The Spanish influence is evident in the use of tomatoes and peppers combined with eggs.

PREPARATION: 15 mins
COOKING: 5 mins

3 eggs
Salt and pepper
1 tbsp butter or margarine
¼ green pepper, cut into small dice
60g/2oz ham, cut into small dice
2 tomatoes, peeled, seeded and roughly
    chopped

1. Break the eggs into a bowl, season with salt and pepper and beat to mix thoroughly. Heat an omelette pan and drop in the butter, swirling

Step 2 Push eggs with fork to let the uncooked portion run to the bottom of the pan.

Step 3 Fold a third of the omelette to the middle.

it so that it coats the bottom and sides. When the butter stops foaming, add the pepper and ham. Cook for 1-2 minutes to soften slightly, and add the tomatoes.

2. Pour in the eggs and as they begin to cook, push back the cooked portion with the flat of the fork to allow the uncooked portion to run underneath. Continue to lift the eggs and shake the pan to prevent them from sticking.

3. When the egg on top is still slightly creamy, fold a third of the omelette to the centre and tip it out of the pan onto a warm serving dish, folded side down. Serve immediately.

Lamb Korma

SERVES 1
One of the best known Indian curries, a korma is rich, spicy and a traditional favourite.

PREPARATION: 15 mins
COOKING: 50 mins

½ small onion, sliced
2 tsps vegetable oil
Piece of cinnamon stick
2 cloves
1 cardamom pod
½ bay leaf
¼ tsp black cumin seeds
½ tsp ginger paste, or grated fresh ginger
¼ tsp garlic paste, or 1 small clove garlic, crushed
150g/5oz shoulder of lamb, cubed
¼ tsp chilli powder
¼ tsp ground coriander
½ tsp ground cumin
Pinch of ground turmeric
2 tbsps natural yogurt
90ml/3 fl oz water
Salt to taste
1 tsp ground almonds
½ green chilli, seeded
Fresh coriander leaves, chopped

---

1. Fry the onion in the oil until golden brown. Add the cinnamon, cloves, cardamom, bay leaf and the cumin seeds. Fry for 1 minute.

2. Add the ginger and garlic pastes and the cubed lamb. Sprinkle over the chilli powder, ground coriander, cumin and turmeric and mix together well.

3. Stir in the yogurt, cover the pan and cook over a moderate heat for 10-15 minutes, stirring occasionally.

4. Add the water and salt to taste, re-cover and simmer gently for 30-40 minutes, or until the meat is tender.

5. Just before serving, add the almonds, chilli and coriander leaves. Stir in a little more water if necessary, to produce a medium-thick gravy.

Pan-Blackened Fish

SERVES 1

This Cajun recipe from America uses a spice mixture which is very hot, so use less if you want.

PREPARATION: 15 mins
COOKING: 5 mins

60g/2oz unsalted butter
1 fish steak about 225g/8oz in weight
¾ tsp paprika
¼ tsp garlic granules
¼ tsp cayennne pepper
½ tsp salt and some ground pepper
¼ tsp dried thyme

---

1. Melt the butter, pour about half into a ramekin dish and set aside.

2. Brush the fish steak liberally on both sides with the remaining butter.

3. Mix together the spices, seasoning and thyme and sprinkle generously on each side of the fish, patting it on by hand.

4. Heat a frying pan and add about 15g/½oz

Step 5 Cook the first side until it is very brown then turn over to cook the second side.

butter. When the butter is hot, add the fish.

5. Turn the fish over when the underside is very brown, this should take at least 2 minutes, and repeat with the second side. Add more butter if necessary.

6. Cook until the top side of the fish is very dark brown. Serve the fish immediately with the dish of butter for dipping.

Liver with Onions

SERVES 1

This dish is simple to prepare, but absolutely delicious and highly nutritious.

PREPARATION: 15 mins
COOKING: 10 mins

---

1 small onion
150g/5oz lambs' liver, thinly sliced
Salt and freshly ground black pepper
3 tbsps plain flour
1½ tbsps vegetable oil
15g/½oz butter
2 tsps fresh chopped parsley

---

1. Peel the onion and slice thinly, keeping each slice in circles if possible.

2. Trim away any tubes from the liver using a

Step 1 Peel the onion and slice thinly keeping each slice in circles if possible.

Step 3 Coat the liver slices with seasoned flour.

pair of small scissors or a sharp knife.

3. Mix the seasoning and the flour together on a plate and lay the slices of liver in the flour, turning them and pressing them gently to coat all over evenly.

4. Put the oil and the butter into a large frying pan. Heat gently until foaming.

5. Add the onion rings and fry until just golden.

6. Add the liver slices and fry for 2-3 minutes on each side until just cooked. Cooking time will depend on the thickness of each slice.

7. Stir the parsley into the liver and onions and serve immediately.

Lamb a l'Orange

SERVES 1

The refreshing taste of orange complements lamb beautifully and this recipe is an ideal way of using up leftover lamb.

PREPARATION: 15 mins
COOKING: 18 mins

---

1 tsp oil
1 shallot, finely chopped
1 small orange
1 tsp redcurrant jelly
90ml/3 fl oz stock
Pinch of mustard powder
Pinch of caster sugar
Pinch of cayenne pepper
1 tsp cornflour
175g/6oz cooked lamb

---

1. Heat the oil in a frying pan and sauté the shallot gently until soft but not brown.

2. Grate half the orange rind, cut 3 slices from the orange, trim away the pith and reserve the slices for garnish.

3. Squeeze the juice from the remainder of the orange and add to the shallot, with the orange rind, redcurrant jelly and stock.

Step 2 Cut 3 slices from the orange, trim away the pith and reserve for garnish.

4. Bring this mixture to the boil, reduce the heat and cook, stirring continuously, for 5 minutes.

5. Blend the mustard, sugar, pepper and cornflour together with 2 tsps cold water, and stir this into the orange sauce.

6. Slice the lamb, add this to the sauce and bring to the boil.

7. Reduce the heat and simmer for 10-12 minutes. When cooked, transfer the lamb to a serving dish, pour a little of the sauce over and garnish with the reserved orange slices.

Chicken and Sausage Risotto

SERVES 1
This is really a one-pot meal and one you won't have to cook in the oven.

PREPARATION: 25 mins
COOKING: 25 mins

15g/½oz butter or margarine
½ small onion, roughly chopped
1 stick celery, roughly chopped
½ small green pepper, roughly chopped
1 small clove garlic, crushed
Salt and pepper
60g/2oz uncooked rice
1 small chicken breast, skinned, boned, and cut
  into cubes
90g/3oz canned tomatoes
30g/1oz smoked sausage, cut into 1.25cm/
  ½-inch dice
200ml/7 fl oz chicken stock
Chopped parsley

---

1. Melt the butter or margarine in a large saucepan and add the onion. Cook slowly to brown and then add the celery, green pepper and garlic and cook briefly.

2. Add the salt and pepper and the rice, stirring to mix well. Add the chicken, tomatoes, sausage and stock and mix well.

3. Bring to the boil, then reduce the heat to simmering and cook for about 20-25 minutes, stirring occasionally until the chicken is done and the rice is tender. The rice should have absorbed most of the liquid by the time it has cooked. Stir in some chopped parsley and serve.

Paprika Schnitzel

SERVES 1

Thin slices of fillet pork are served with a rich tasting paprika sauce for a delicious low calorie meal.

PREPARATION: 20 mins
COOKING: 15 mins

2 thin slices fillet pork, cut along the fillet
Salt and freshly ground black pepper
1 small clove garlic, crushed
2 tsps vegetable oil
½ small onion
½ small red pepper
½ small green pepper
¾ tsp paprika
3 tbsps beef stock
2 tbsps red wine
2 tsps tomato purée
3 tbsps natural yogurt

Step 1 Flatten the pork fillets with a rolling pin until 5mm/¼-inch thick.

1. Trim the slices of pork to remove any fat,

and flatten them out with a rolling pin until they are 5mm/¼-inch thick.

2. Rub both sides of the pork fillets with salt, pepper and garlic, then allow to stand in a refrigerator for 30 minutes.

3. Heat the oil in a large frying pan and cook the pork fillets until they are well browned and cooked right through. This will take about 4 minutes for each side.

4. Remove the pork from the pan, set aside, and keep warm.

5. Thinly slice the onion and the peppers. Add to the oil and meat juices in the frying pan, and cook quickly for about 3-4 minutes until they are soft but not browned.

6. Add the paprika, stock, wine and tomato purée to the frying pan with the vegetables, and bring the mixture to the boil.

7. Reduce the heat and simmer until the liquid has evaporated and the sauce has thickened. Season with salt and pepper to taste.

8. Arrange the pork slices on a serving dish and pour the paprika sauce over the top.

9. Beat the yogurt until it is smooth and carefully drizzle over the paprika sauce to make an attractive pattern. Serve hot.

Crunchy Cod

SERVES 1

Cod provides the perfect base for a crunchy, slightly spicy topping.

PREPARATION: 15 mins
COOKING: 12 mins

---

1 cod fillet
Salt and pepper
30g/1oz butter, melted
30g/1oz dry breadcrumbs
¼ tsp mustard powder
¼ tsp crushed garlic
Dash of Worcestershire sauce and Tabasco
½ tbsp lemon juice
1 tsp finely chopped parsley

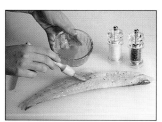

Step 1 Season the fish fillet then brush with melted butter.

Step 3 Press the crumbs on gently to pack them in place.

1. Season the fish fillet with salt and pepper and place on a grill pan. Brush with some of the butter and cook under a medium preheated grill for about 5 minutes.

2. Combine the remaining butter with the breadcrumbs, mustard, garlic, Worcestershire sauce, Tabasco, lemon juice and parsley.

3. Spoon the mixture carefully on top of the fish fillet, covering it completely. Press down lightly to pack the crumbs into place. Grill for a further 5-7 minutes, or until the top is lightly browned and the fish flakes easily.

Corned Beef Hash

SERVES 1
The addition of cooked beetroot gives this dish a dash of colour.

PREPARATION: 20 mins
COOKING: 30 mins

175g/6oz canned corned beef
1 medium boiled potato, roughly chopped
½ small onion, finely chopped
Salt, pepper and nutmeg
1 medium cooked beetroot, peeled and diced
1 tbsp oil

---

1. Cut the corned beef into small pieces.

Step 2 Add the meat mixture to the pan and spread it out evenly in the pan.

Step 4 When a crust forms on the bottom, turn the mixture over to brown the other side.

Combine with all the remaining ingredients except the oil.

2. Melt the oil in a frying pan and, when hot, add the meat mixture. Spread it out evenly in the pan.

3. Cook over low heat, pressing the mixture down continuously with a wooden spoon or fish slice. Cook for about 15-20 minutes.

4. When a crust forms on the bottom, turn over and brown the other side. Serve on its own or top with a poached egg.

Piquant Pork Chop

SERVES 1

The spicy sauce in this recipe completely transforms the humble pork chop.

PREPARATION: 15 mins
COOKING: 40 mins

---

1 lean pork chop, trimmed of fat and rind
Oil
½ small onion, chopped
1 tsp brown sugar
½-1 tsp mustard powder
½ tsp tomato purée
½ beef stock cube
140ml/¼ pint water
½ tsp Worcestershire sauce
1½ tbsps fresh lemon juice

---

1. Grill the pork chop under a preheated hot grill for 6-7 minutes on each side.

2. Heat a little oil in a small frying pan, and sauté the onion gently until it is lightly browned.

3. Stir the sugar, mustard powder, tomato purée and beef stock cube into the cooked onion. Mix the ingredients together well, then add the water and bring to the boil, stirring continuously.

4. Stir the Worcestershire sauce and the lemon juice into the onion and spice mixture, then check the seasoning, adding freshly ground sea salt and black pepper to taste.

5. Put the pork chop into a small ovenproof baking dish and pour the sauce over.

6. Cook in a preheated oven at 180°C/350°F/Gas Mark 4, for about 40-45 minutes, or until the meat is tender.

Gammon Steaks with Raisin Sauce

SERVES 1

The tart and sweet flavour of this sauce is the perfect choice to complement gammon.

PREPARATION: 30 mins
COOKING: 15 mins

---

2 small gammon steaks, cut about 5mm/¼-inch
thick
Milk
Oil or butter for frying

Sauce
1 tsp cornflour
90ml/6 tbsps cider
Large pinch of ground ginger or allspice
1 tsp lemon juice
15g/½ oz raisins
Pinch of salt

---

1. Soak the steaks in enough milk to barely cover for 30 minutes. Rinse and dry. Trim off the rind and snip the edges of the steaks.

2. Heat a small amount of oil or butter in a large frying pan and brown the steaks for about 2 minutes per side over a medium-high heat.

Step 1 Snip the edges of the gammon steaks to prevent the slices from curling.

3. Mix the cornflour with about 1 tbsp of the cider and deglaze the frying pan with the remaining cider. Stir in the ginger or allspice and the lemon juice.

4. Stirring constantly, pour in the cornflour mixture and bring the liquid to the boil. Cook and stir constantly until thickened.

5. Add the raisins and cook for a further 5 minutes. Add salt to taste. Reheat the gammon quickly, if necessary, and pour the sauce over the steaks to serve.

Lamb in a Parcel

SERVES 1

Use this quick and easy recipe to make a whole meal in one convenient parcel.

PREPARATION: 15 mins
COOKING: 1 hour

Oil
1 lamb steak or 2 rib chops
1 potato, scrubbed
2 baby carrots, scraped
½ small onion, sliced
½ small green pepper, sliced
½ tsp dill seeds
Salt and pepper

---

1. Heat a frying pan and add a small amount of oil. Quickly fry the lamb on both sides to sear and brown.

Step 5 Top the lamb with the onion and pepper slices.

Step 6 Sprinkle with dill, salt and pepper and seal the foil into a parcel.

2. Cut a piece of foil about 30 × 45cm/12 × 18 inches and oil lightly.

3. Cut the potato in half and place on the piece of foil, cut side up.

4. Top with the lamb and place the carrots on either side.

5. Place the onion slices on the lamb and the pepper slices on top of the onions.

6. Sprinkle with the dill, salt and pepper, and seal the foil into a parcel.

7. Bake in an oven preheated to 200°C/400°F/ Gas Mark 6, for about 45 minutes-1 hour, or until the potato is tender and the meat is cooked. Open the parcel at the table.

Sautéed Lemon Pork

SERVES 1

A perfect way to prepare this tender cut of pork. Butchers will bat out the meat for you.

PREPARATION: 25 mins
COOKING: 25 mins

---

2 small pork escalopes or steaks, batted out
    until thin
Flour for dredging
Salt and pepper
15g/½oz butter or margarine
½ small green pepper, thinly sliced
1 small lemon
1½ tbsps dry white wine or sherry
3 tbsps chicken stock

---

1. Dust the pork with a mixture of flour, salt and pepper. Shake off the excess.

2. Melt the butter or margarine in a frying pan and brown the pork. Remove the meat and keep it warm.

3. Add the pepper to the pan and cook briefly, then set aside with the pork.

4. Cut the lemon in half and squeeze 2 tsps juice from one half. Cut all the peel and pith off the other half and thinly slice the flesh.

5. Pour the wine or sherry and lemon juice into the pan to deglaze. Add the stock and bring to the boil. Boil for 2-3 minutes to reduce.

6. Add the pork and peppers and cook for 10-15 minutes over gentle heat. Add the lemon slices and heat through before serving.

Beef with Broccoli

SERVES 1

This recipe uses the traditional Chinese method of cutting meat for stir-frying which ensures that the meat will be tender and will cook quickly.

PREPARATION: 25 mins
COOKING: 4 mins

175g/6oz rump steak, partially frozen
60ml/4 tbsps dark soy sauce
1 tbsp cornflour
1 tbsp dry sherry
1 tsp sugar
90g/3oz fresh broccoli
1.25cm/½-inch piece ginger, peeled and
   shredded
3 tbsps oil
Salt and pepper

---

1. Trim any fat from the meat and cut into very thin strips across the grain – the strips should be about 7.5cm/3 inches long.

2. Combine the meat with the soy sauce,

Step 1 Cut the meat into thin strips across the grain.

Step 3 Cut the peeled broccoli stalks into thin diagonal slices.

cornflour, sherry and sugar. Stir well and leave long enough for the meat to completely defrost.

3. Trim the florets from the stalks of the broccoli and cut them into even-sized pieces. Peel the stalks of the broccoli and cut into thin, diagonal slices.

4. Slice the ginger into shreds. Heat a wok and add half of the oil to it. Add the broccoli and sprinkle with salt. Stir-fry, turning constantly, until the broccoli is dark green. Do not cook for longer than 2 minutes. Remove from the wok and set aside.

5. Place the remaining oil in the wok and add the ginger and beef. Stir-fry, turning constantly, for about 2 minutes. Return the broccoli to the pan and mix well. Heat through for 30 seconds and serve immediately.

Apple Filled Pancake

SERVES 1

A light, puffy pancake makes a delicious brunch dish as well as a sweet.

PREPARATION: 15 mins
COOKING: 15 mins

Filling
15g/½oz butter or margarine
1 cooking apple, peeled, cored and cut into
   5 mm/¼-inch wedges
1 tsp brown sugar
Pinch of ground allspice

Pancake
1 egg
120ml/4 fl oz milk
15g/½oz plain flour
¼ tsp sugar
Pinch of salt
15g/½oz butter or margarine
Icing sugar

---

1. Melt the butter for the filling in a small frying pan over moderate heat. When just foaming, add the apple and sprinkle with the sugar and allspice. Cook, stirring occasionally, until the apple is lightly browned and slightly softened. Put the apple aside while preparing the batter.

2. Combine the egg and the milk in a bowl and whisk thoroughly. Sift the flour with the sugar and salt and add to the egg gradually, whisking

Step 4 Scatter the apple filling evenly over the pancake.

constantly. Alternatively, combine all the ingredients in a food processor and work until just smooth.

3. To cook the pancake, melt the butter over moderate heat in a 15cm/6-inch frying pan. Pour in half the batter and swirl the pan from side to side so that the batter covers the base.

4. Scatter over the filling and cook the pancake for about 3 minutes.

5. Pour the rest of the batter over the apples and place under a preheated grill for about 1-2 minutes, or until the top is golden brown and firm to the touch.

6. Loosen the sides and the base of the pancake and slide it onto a heated serving dish. Sprinkle the pancake with a little icing sugar.

Brown Sugar Banana

SERVES 1

Banana cooked in a rich brown sugar sauce makes a delectable dessert.

PREPARATION: 10 mins
COOKING: 8 mins

---

1 ripe banana, peeled
Lemon juice
30g/1oz butter
30g/1oz soft brown sugar, light or dark
Pinch of ground cinnamon and nutmeg
2 tbsps orange juice
1 tbsp white or dark rum
Whipped cream and chopped pecans, to serve

1. Cut the banana in half lengthwise and sprinkle with lemon juice on all sides.

2. Melt the butter in a small frying pan and add the sugar, cinnamon, nutmeg and orange juice. Stir over gentle heat until the sugar dissolves into a syrup.

3. Add the banana halves and cook gently for about 3 minutes, basting often with the syrup, but not turning them.

4. Once the banana is heated through, warm the rum in a small saucepan or ladle and ignite with a match. Pour the flaming rum over the banana and shake the pan gently until the flames die down naturally. Place on a serving plate and top with some whipped cream and a sprinkling of pecans.

Brioche French Toast

SERVES 1

This brioche French toast can be served as an unusual dessert, and also as an extra-special breakfast dish, with or without vanilla custard sauce.

PREPARATION: 5 mins
COOKING: 4 mins

---

1 small brioche
1 tbsp double cream
1 small egg
1 tsp sugar
¼ tsp orange flower water
2 tbsps butter
Icing sugar
Vanilla custard sauce, to serve

---

1. Cut the small brioche into three slices.

2. Beat together the cream, egg, sugar, and orange flower water.

3. Dip each brioche slice into the cream and egg mixture, making sure both sides are coated.

4. Heat a little butter and sauté the dipped slices in a frying pan for about 2 minutes on each side until golden brown.

Step 3 Dip each brioche slice into the cream and egg mixture, coating both sides.

Step 4 Sauté the dipped slices for about 2 minutes on each side until golden.

5. Serve immediately, sprinkled with a little sifted icing sugar and surrounded by the vanilla custard sauce.

Index

Apple Filled Pancake 38
Beef with Broccoli 36
Brioche French Toast 42
Brown Sugar Banana 40
Chicken and Sausage Risotto 20
Corned Beef Hash 26
Crunchy Cod 24
Desserts:
    Apple Filled Pancake 38
    Brioche French Toast 42
    Brown Sugar Banana 40
Gammon Steaks with Raisin Sauce 30
Lamb a l'Orange 18
Lamb in a Parcel 32
Lamb Korma 12
Liver with Onions 14
Lunches and Suppers:
    Beef with Broccoli 36
    Corned Beef Hash 26
    Crunchy Cod 24

Liver with Onions 16
Omelette Rousillon 10
Scrambled Eggs with Olives 8
Main Courses:
    Chicken and Sausage Risotto 20
    Gammon Steaks with Raisin
        Sauce 30
    Lamb a l'Orange 18
    Lamb in a Parcel 32
    Lamb Korma 12
    Pan-Blackened Fish 16
    Paprika Schnitzel 22
    Piquant Pork Chop 28
    Sautéed Lemon Pork 34
Omelette Rousillon 10
Pan-Blackened Fish 14
Paprika Schnitzel 22
Piquant Pork Chop 28
Sautéed Lemon Pork 34
Scrambled Eggs with Olives 8